The Taking Action Guide to Building Coherence in Schools, Districts, and Systems

To coherence makers who change the world

—Michael

To my family, who continue to give me roots and wings

—Joanne

To Lilly, my source of inspiration and joy: may you be a lifelong learner

—Eleanor

The Taking Action Guide to Building Coherence in Schools, Districts, and Systems

Michael Fullan

Joanne Quinn

Eleanor Adam

A Joint Publication

ONTARIO PRINCIPALS' COUNCIL
Exemplary Leadership in Public Education

CORWIN
A SAGE Publishing Company

FOR INFORMATION:

Corwin

A SAGE Company

2455 Teller Road

Thousand Oaks, California 91320

(800) 233-9936

www.corwin.com

SAGE Publications Ltd.

1 Oliver's Yard

55 City Road

London EC1Y 1SP

United Kingdom

SAGE Publications India Pvt. Ltd.

B 1/I 1 Mohan Cooperative Industrial Area

Mathura Road, New Delhi 110 044

India

SAGE Publications Asia-Pacific Pte Ltd

18 Cross Street #10-10/11/12

China Square Central

Singapore 048423

Executive Editor: Arnis Burvikovs

Senior Associate Editor: Desirée A. Bartlett

Senior Editorial Assistant: Andrew Olson

Production Editor: Melanie Birdsall

Copy Editor: Diana Breti

Typesetter: C&M Digitals (P) Ltd.

Proofreader: Alison Syring

Cover Designer: Janet Kiesel

Marketing Manager: Anna Mesick

Copyright © 2016 by Corwin

Printed in the United States of America

Library of Congress Cataloging-in-Publication Data

Names: Fullan, Michael, author. | Quinn, Joanne, author. | Adam, Eleanor, author.

Title: The taking action guide to building coherence in schools, districts, and systems / Michael Fullan, Joanne Quinn, Eleanor Adam.

Description: Thousand Oaks, California : Corwin, a SAGE company, 2016. | Includes bibliographical references (p.).

Identifiers: LCCN 2016006997 | ISBN 9781506350271 (pbk. : alk. paper)

Subjects: LCSH: Educational change—United States—Handbooks, manuals, etc. | Educational planning—United States—Handbooks, manuals, etc. | School improvement programs—United States—Handbooks, manuals, etc. | Educational leadership—United States—Handbooks, manuals, etc.

Classification: LCC LA217.2 .F86 2016 | DDC 370.973—dc23

LC record available at https://lccn.loc.gov/2016006997

This book is printed on acid-free paper.

SUSTAINABLE FORESTRY INITIATIVE

Certified Chain of Custody

At Least 10% Certified Forest Content

www.sfiprogram.org

SFI-01028

16 17 18 19 20 10 9 8 7 6 5 4 3 2

Contents

Preface   vii

How to Use This Guide   viii

Overview of the Modules   xi

Chapter 1. Coherence Making   1

  1. Quote Walkabout Protocol   2

  2. Say Something Protocol   5

  3. What? So What? Now What? Protocol   6

  4. Video Jigsaw Protocol   7

  5. Coherence Framework Assessment Protocol   9

Chapter 2. Focusing Direction   10

  6. Quick Write Protocol   11

  7. Video and Slide the Line Protocol   13

  8. Reduce, Reframe, Remove Protocol   14

  9. Change Quality Quadrant Protocol   17

 10. Carousel Brainstorming Protocol   18

 11. Turn and Talk Protocol   20

 12. Think-Pair-Share Protocol   21

 13. Both Sides Now Protocol   22

 14. Integration Inventory Protocol   23

Chapter 3. Cultivating Collaborative Cultures   26

 15. Concept Attainment Protocol   27

 16. Video Viewing Advance Organizer Protocol   28

 17. Four A's Protocol   30

 18. Lead Learner Competencies Protocol   31

 19. Reciprocal Teaching Protocol   32

 20. Sticky Note Clustering Protocol   34

 21. Read, Record, Retell, Relate, and Reflect Protocol   36

Chapter 4. Deepening Learning   38

22. Affinity Protocol   39
23. 6Cs Protocol   40
24. Through the Looking Glass Protocol   43
25. Shifting Instructional Practices Protocol   45
26. Instructional Coherence Framework Protocol   47

Chapter 5. Securing Accountability   49

27. Three-Step Interview Protocol   50

Chapter 6. Leading for Coherence   54

28. Check for Understanding Protocol   55
29. Reviewing Leadership Plan Protocol: Part A   57
30. Reviewing Leadership Plan Protocol: Part B   58

Chapter 7. Mastering the Framework   60

31. Taking Action Protocol   61
32. Coherence Progression Protocol   63
33. Coherence Planning Protocol   73

References   75

About the Authors   76

Preface

"It is time to make good on the promise of public education. Our children need it, the public is demanding it, and indeed the world needs it to survive and thrive" (Fullan & Quinn, 2015, p. 1).

Now is the time to focus on coherence! But *how* do you build the much-needed coherence?

The book *Coherence: The Right Drivers in Action for Schools, Districts, and Systems* is all about regular school systems achieving remarkable results by focusing on the right things and staying with them. *The Taking Action Guide* is intended to help you become one of those successful systems that makes a difference for all students.

Incorporated in *The Taking Action Guide to Building Coherence in Schools, Districts, and Systems* are protocols for each chapter of the book *Coherence: The Right Drivers in Action for Schools, Districts, and Systems*. The protocols provide staff with common learning experiences and promote deep discussion, encourage critical thinking about the coherence in the organization, and, as a result, build capacity. The protocols serve as building blocks to develop ongoing and specific actions. Once participants understand the Coherence Framework in their context, they are able to analyze the level of coherence in the organization and to *take action* by developing a 100-Day Plan to foster greater coherence.

But first, before you start, read *Coherence: The Right Drivers in Action for Schools, Districts, and Systems*. Tools help you focus, but only if you have good ideas. Get some ideas from the book and then get to action and learn more.

Focus and coherence has never been more badly needed. Now is the time for action.

How to Use This Guide

*T*he *Taking Action Guide to Building Coherence in Schools, Districts, and Systems* provides organizations with step-by-step experiences to build the knowledge and skills needed to foster greater coherence.

Getting Started

Selecting Participants

The context of your organization will determine whom you select, but the following have been successful in a range of organizations:

1. **Role-Alike Study Groups.** Provide a professional learning opportunity for a particular role to build capacity around coherence and the use of the right drivers (e.g., all school administrators, a district leadership team, state superintendents study group). A book study incorporating the protocols promotes powerful learning and dialogue and will lead to greater coherence.

2. **Vertical Coherence Team.** Organize a cross-role group composed of representatives of all levels of the organization. In school districts, this might include district staff, school administrators, union representatives, and others, while at state or provincial level, this might include state superintendents, key leaders of the DOE, association leaders, union leaders, and district leaders. Leaders who learn together are more likely to be committed to the tasks and to actualizing a plan of action. We strongly recommend that you keep the team consistent throughout the process, to move from analysis to action. This provides an opportunity to learn from the work as participants build upon prior learning, share differing perspectives, and engage in deep dialogue. Developing a trusting team is critical and is enhanced through the protocols and your choice of community builders.

Role of Participants

Participants have six key roles as part of the team:

- Represent a range of perspectives
- Communicate with stakeholder groups
- Share expertise

- Be transparent
- Participate fully
- Develop a draft plan for coherence

Sharing and then gaining participants' commitment to perform the roles is an important first step in the process. It is also helpful to review at the conclusion of each session the responsibilities of each member for the next meeting.

Role of Facilitator

Critical to the success of *The Taking Action Guide* is a facilitator who serves not only as a lead learner but also does the following:

- clarifies the purpose of the work together: analyzing district coherence, mastering the framework, and developing the 100-Day Plan to achieve greater coherence in the organization
- establishes a set of norms for working together
- organizes the sessions: dates, times, locations
- understands and implements the protocols for each session
- provides necessary resources
- encourages participation by all
- helps to resolve issues or conflicts
- records decisions
- communicates regularly with team members and other stakeholders

Format

To begin, all participants should read *Coherence: The Right Drivers in Action for Schools, Districts, and Systems.* Facilitators should select the most relevant protocols to meet the needs of their group and ensure adequate time for deep dialogue.

The sequence of and timing of sessions can range from a one- or two-hour study group for each chapter to full day or retreat sessions.

Using the Protocols

Protocols are provided for each chapter. Each protocol contributes to an assessment of the organization's current level of coherence using the Coherence Progressions and the 100-Day Plan to achieve greater coherence.

Each protocol provides

- a purpose,
- links to video and print resources,
- a description of the protocol,
- the directions for using the protocol, and
- the required advance organizers.

For each protocol, participants will read and discuss the specific chapter of the book as well as read additional appropriate articles or view videos. This common learning experience ensures the dialogue will be richer and more meaningful.

Each protocol is described in detail and includes powerful instructional strategies to encourage the interaction between colleagues. The infographics found at the end of each chapter in *Coherence* assist in capturing the concepts and are a means to summarize your decisions and actions as you progress through the book. As you proceed through the book and implement the protocols, there are many opportunities to connect to your organization's reality.

In the final section of *The Taking Action Guide*, three protocols serve as stepping stones to build coherence and require both individual and collective reflection and action.

The Taking Action Protocols are reflection and planning tools at the conclusion of each chapter; these allow participants to reflect individually and collectively during and between sessions.

The Coherence Progression Protocol is a diagnostic and planning tool. It provides a detailed guide for analyzing each of the four components of the Coherence Framework. The progression describes organizations at three levels of development: emerging, accelerating, and mastering. Using the progression, participants reflect on the current level of coherence in their school, district, or state and then plan steps that will lead to the next level of coherence.

The Coherence Planning Protocol provides an organizer for synthesizing the results developed by the Taking Action Protocols at the end of each chapter. This plan for increasing coherence includes specific actions for the next 100 days.

Most of us in education need greater coherence in our work. Use the Coherence Framework and *The Taking Action Guide* to take collection action. It is the time to develop shared coherence. This guide will help you do just that.

Overview of the Modules

Module	Purpose	Content	Protocol
Chapter 1 **Coherence Making**	Builds understanding of the key concepts of coherence and a pre-assessment of the four components	Coherence Defined	Quote Walkabout
		Change Drivers	Say Something What? So What? Now What?
		The Coherence Framework	Video Jigsaw Assessment
Chapter 2 **Focusing Direction**	Examines and builds shared purpose	Purpose Driven	Quick Write Slide the Line
	Provides a protocol to focus goals and tackle overload and fragmentation	Goals That Impact	Reduce, Reframe, Remove
	Provides a way to assess the explicitness of strategy and change climate	Clarity of Strategy	Change Quality Quadrant
	Provides three change approaches to support people during the change process	Change Leadership—Shifting Practice	Carousel Brainstorming
		Change Leadership—Push and Pull	Turn and Talk Think-Pair-Share Both Sides Now
		Change Leadership—Capacity and Integration	Integration Inventory
Chapter 3 **Cultivating Collaborative Cultures**	Deepens understanding of a growth mind-set in organizations	Growth Mind-Set	Concept Attainment
	Provides opportunities to examine and self-assess the components of learning leadership	Learning Leadership	Video Viewing Advance Organizer Four A's Lead Learner Competencies

(Continued)

(Continued)

Module	Purpose	Content	Protocol
Chapter 3 **Cultivating Collaborative Cultures** *(Continued)*	Deepens the understanding of capacity building and impact	Capacity Building Criteria and Impact	Reciprocal Teaching
	Examines protocols for meaningful collaborative work	Shifting the Organization	Sticky Note Clustering
		Collaborative Work in Action	Read, Record, Retell, Relate, and Reflect
Chapter 4 **Deepening Learning**	Provides a process for clarifying learning goals and understanding deep learning competencies	Clarity of Learning Goals	Affinity 6Cs
	Provides a protocol for building common language, instructional practices, and an instructional coherence framework	Precision in Pedagogy	Through the Looking Glass Shifting Instructional Practices Instructional Coherence Framework
Chapter 5 **Securing Accountability**	Builds understanding of the power of internal and external accountability	Internal and External Accountability	Three-Step Interview
Chapter 6 **Leading for Coherence**	Deepens understanding of the importance of leadership at all levels and a strategy for planning	Developing Leaders	Check for Understanding Reviewing Leadership Plan
Chapter 7 **Mastering the Framework**	Provides action prompts to guide discussion and decisions at the end of each chapter	Synthesizing Actions for Each Chapter	Taking Action
	Provides a progression for assessing the current degree of coherence in the school or district	Assessing Coherence	Coherence Progression
	Provides a format for strategizing and capturing a plan for increasing coherence	Strategizing for Action	Coherence Planning

Chapter 1

Coherence Making

1. Quote Walkabout Protocol   2

2. Say Something Protocol   5

3. What? So What? Now What? Protocol   6

4. Video Jigsaw Protocol   7

5. Coherence Framework Assessment Protocol   9

1. Quote Walkabout Protocol

Purpose

- Review the key ideas for making coherence.
- Clarify the definition of coherence.

Link

Reading: Pages ix–16 from *Coherence: The Right Drivers in Action for Schools, Districts, and Systems,* by Michael Fullan and Joanne Quinn (Corwin, 2015).

Quote Walkabout Protocol

The Quote Walkabout Protocol introduces a particular topic. Individuals select quotes that resonate for them and discuss the quotes with peers.

1. Read the quotes and select two quotes that resonate with you.

2. Record your quotes on the advance organizer.

3. Share your reflections with a colleague and compare choices.

4. Repeat with a second partner.

5. With your second partner, define *coherence* as it applies to your school/district.

1. Quote Walkabout Protocol (Continued)

"There is only one way to achieve greater coherence, and that is through purposeful action and interaction, working on capacity, clarity, precision of practice, transparency, monitoring of progress, and continuous correction. All of this requires the right mixture of 'pressure and support': the press for progress within supportive and focused cultures." (page 2)	
"Coherence making in other words is a continuous process of making and remaking meaning in your own mind and in your culture. Our framework shows you how to do this." (page 3)	
"*Effective change processes shape and reshape good ideas as they build capacity and ownership among participants.* There are two components: the quality of the idea and the quality of the process." (page 14)	
" . . . that these highly successful organizations learned from the success of others but never tried to imitate what others did. Instead, they found *their own pathway to success.* They did many of the right things, and they learned and adjusted as they proceeded." (page 15)	

Coherence Defined

Coherence Defined

1. Quote Walkabout Protocol (Continued)

"Most people would rather be challenged by change and helped to progress than be mired in frustration. Best of all, this work tackles 'whole systems' and uses the group to change the group. People know they are engaged in something beyond their narrow role. It is human nature to rise to a larger call *if* the problems are serious enough and *if* there is a way forward where they can play a role with others. Coherence making is the pathway that does this." (page ix)	
"What we need is consistency of purpose, policy, and practice. Structure and strategy are not enough. The solution requires the individual and collective ability to build shared meaning, capacity, and commitment to action. When large numbers of people have a deeply understood sense of what needs to be done— and see their part in achieving that purpose— coherence emerges and powerful things happen." (page 1)	
"Coherence pertains to people individually and especially collectively. To cut to the chase, coherence consists of the shared depth of understanding about the purpose and nature of the work. Coherence, then, is what is in the minds and actions of people individually and especially collectively." (pages 1–2)	

2. Say Something Protocol

Purpose

- Understand the right and wrong drivers of change.

Link

Reading: "Choosing the Wrong Drivers for Whole System Reform," by Michael Fullan (Centre for Strategic Education, April 2011). Available at http://www.michaelfullan.ca/media/13396088160.pdf

Say Something Protocol

Say Something is a paired reading protocol designed to increase individual and shared understanding of concepts and foster conversation to deepen understanding between two participants who are working collaboratively (Short, Burke, & Harste, 1995).

1. With a partner, decide on a midway break in the article.

2. Read independently the first section, highlighting key ideas or questions you may have.

3. Stop midway and use the Reflecting Prompts for your dialogue.

4. Use the Reflecting Prompts again at the conclusion of the article.

Reflecting Prompts

- Summarize your thinking about the reading.
- Identify key points.
- Make a connection to your own work.
- Share thinking about a new idea.
- Raise a question about a concept or strategy.

....

3. What? So What? Now What? Protocol

....

Purpose

- Apply the right drivers concepts to your school/district.

Link

Reading: "Choosing the Wrong Drivers for Whole System Reform," by Michael Fullan (Centre for Strategic Education, April 2011). Available at http://www.michaelfullan.ca/media/13396088160.pdf

What? So What? Now What? Protocol

The What? So What? Now What? Protocol is used to summarize content, to think critically about the implications, and to consider actions to be taken (Borton, 1970).

1. Form a group of four to discuss and deepen your thinking of the above article.

2. Discuss each of the questions on the advance organizer and record your collective ideas.

What? Synthesize the key concepts.	
So What? What are the implications of these concepts?	
Now What? What should we do differently?	

4. Video Jigsaw Protocol

Purpose

- Review the components of the Coherence Framework in action.

Links

District Video Resource: "Peel District School Board," available at https://youtu.be/JV2HYL-WB24

School Video Resource: Central Peel Secondary School, "The Perfect Storm," available at http://www.michaelfullan.ca/ontario-central-peel

Video Jigsaw Protocol

Viewing real-life situations provides a greater understanding of a concept. Using the Video Jigsaw Protocol, each participant becomes an expert on a particular component of the video and takes notes for teaching back to peers.

1. Form a group of four and assign one of the quadrants to each member of the group.

2. Record evidence of your assigned quadrant on the advance organizer.

3. Share your observations.

4. Discuss the role of the leader in building coherence.

The Coherence Framework

Source: Graphic by Taryn Hauritz.

4. Video Jigsaw Protocol (Continued)

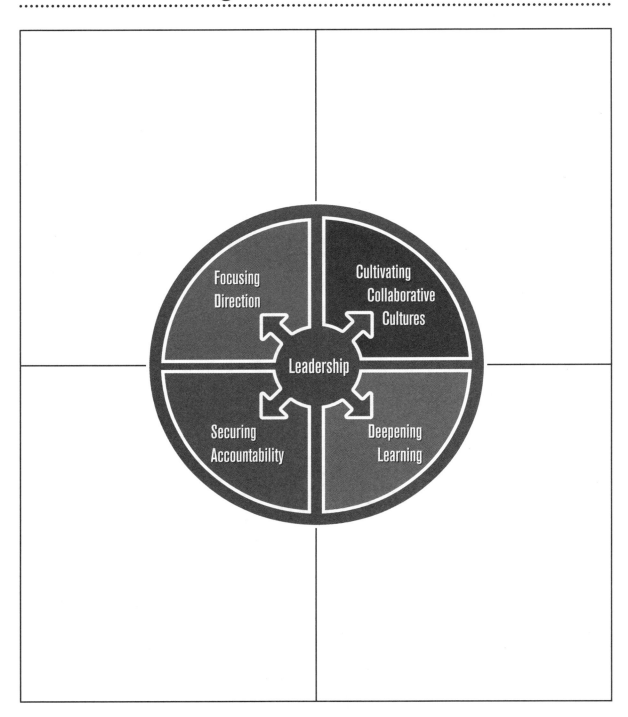

Source: Graphic by Taryn Hauritz.

5. Coherence Framework Assessment Protocol

Purpose

- Use the Coherence Framework Assessment Protocol to assess the degree of coherence in your school/district.

Coherence Framework Assessment Protocol

1. As a school or district team, review the Coherence Framework Assessment Protocol.

2. Provide evidence for the statements as an assessment of your school or district's degree of coherence.

Component		Evidence
Focusing Direction	<ul><li>Shared purpose drives action.</li><li>A small number of goals tied to student learning drives decisions.</li><li>A clear strategy for achieving the goals is known by all.</li><li>Change knowledge is used to move the district forward.</li></ul>	
Cultivating Collaborative Cultures	<ul><li>A growth mind-set underlies the culture.</li><li>Leaders model learning themselves and shape a culture of learning.</li><li>Collective capacity building is fostered above individual development.</li><li>Structures and processes support intentional collaborative work.</li></ul>	
Deepening Learning	<ul><li>Learning goals are clear to everyone and drive instruction.</li><li>A set of effective pedagogical practices is known and used by all educators.</li><li>Robust processes, such as collaborative inquiry and examining student work, are used regularly to improve practice.</li></ul>	
Securing Accountability	<ul><li>Educators take responsibility for continuously improving results.</li><li>Underperformance is an opportunity for growth, not blame.</li><li>External accountability is used transparently to benchmark progress.</li></ul>	

Chapter 2

Focusing Direction

6. Quick Write Protocol   11

7. Video and Slide the Line Protocol   13

8. Reduce, Reframe, Remove Protocol   14

9. Change Quality Quadrant Protocol   17

10. Carousel Brainstorming Protocol   18

11. Turn and Talk Protocol   20

12. Think-Pair-Share Protocol   21

13. Both Sides Now Protocol   22

14. Integration Inventory Protocol   23

6. Quick Write Protocol

Purpose Driven

Purpose

- Examine and articulate the moral purpose.

Link

Reading: Pages 17–24 from *Coherence: The Right Drivers in Action for Schools, Districts, and Systems,* by Michael Fullan and Joanne Quinn (Corwin, 2015).

Leaders need the ability to develop shared moral purpose and meaning as well as a clear strategy for attaining that purpose. The development of shared purpose is a process that sharpens focus while building motivation and commitment. Leaders must understand their own moral purpose before they can develop it in others.

Quick Write Protocol

Quick Write is a protocol that fosters deeper reflection while articulating thinking in written form (Green, Smith, & Brown, 2007; Nunan, 2003).

1. Clarify your own moral purpose by completing the Quick Write worksheet.

   - What is my moral purpose?
   - What actions do I take to realize this moral purpose?
   - How do I help others clarify their moral purpose?
   - Am I making progress in realizing my moral purpose with students?

2. Share your reflections with other members of your team and discuss themes that emerge.

6. Quick Write Protocol (Continued)

What is my moral purpose?
What actions do I take to realize this moral purpose?
How do I help others clarify their moral purpose?
Am I making progress in realizing my moral purpose with students?

7. Video and Slide the Line Protocol

Purpose

- Investigate strategies to engage others in building shared purpose and direction.
- Identify the core focus for your school or district.

Link

Video: "Be the Change That You Want to See in This World," available at https://www.youtube.com/watch?v=nGyutkBvN2s

Slide the Line Protocol

The Slide the Line Protocol fosters deep conversations between participants who may have different viewpoints. It allows for several partners so that an issue or challenge can be discussed from a variety of perspectives.

1. View the video "Be the Change That You Want to See in This World," and while viewing, consider the question, "What helped this group to accomplish a seemingly impossible task?"

2. Share individual reflections on the key elements that contributed to the success of this group.

3. Pair up and form two lines, with partners facing each other (i.e., row A facing row B).

4. Round 1: facing pairs discuss the first prompt. After 2 to 3 minutes, the first person in row A will move to the end of row A, and each person moves one to the right until everyone has a new partner.

5. Rotate for each new prompt.

Prompts
• What is your "tree"? • How do you engage others in moving the tree? • How does this video relate to your moral purpose?

8. Reduce, Reframe, Remove Protocol

Purpose

- Identify a core focus or direction for the school or district.
- Examine a strategy to tackle overload and fragmentation.
- Apply the Three R's—Reduce, Reframe, Remove—Protocol to a school or district.

Link

Reading: Pages 19–27 from *Coherence: The Right Drivers in Action for Schools, Districts, and Systems,* by Michael Fullan and Joanne Quinn (Corwin, 2015).

"The problem is not the absence of goals in schools and districts today but the presence of too many that are ad hoc, unconnected, and ever-changing. Multiple mandates from states and districts combine with the allure of grants and innovations to create overload and fragmentation" (page 19).

Overload results from too many goals, projects, and initiatives. Even when the ideas are good, the sheer volume makes it impossible to implement them.

Fragmentation occurs because even when the goals are the right ones, they may not be experienced by the users as connected ideas. People see them as discrete demands with little connection to each other or their daily work. Implementing too many directions without a coherent sense of how they connect results in paralysis and frustration.

Distractors may arise from competing priorities that are impossible to manage, overwhelming mandates and bureaucratic demands, or alluring innovations. They take attention, time, and resources away from the core focus and goals.

Reduce, Reframe, Remove Protocol

This protocol enables groups to capture a wide range of information or data and organize it into meaningful categories. It builds ownership of the process because each participant first contributes ideas individually and then participates in group analysis of the data generated. It fosters deep discussion, analysis, synthesis, and solution finding.

This three-step process is a vehicle to

- **Reduce** the overload of too many initiatives by decreasing the volume and the overlap of competing directions in order to focus on identifying a small number of core goals;
- **Reframe** the connections and integration of the initiatives or programs that support the small number of goals to avoid fragmentation; and
- **Remove** distractors that take time from the important goals.

8. Reduce, Reframe, Remove Protocol (Continued)

Part A: Reduce

1. Record all the school or district initiatives and programs on sticky notes—one idea per sticky note.

2. Display all sticky notes on a wall or chart paper and discuss each initiative or program to develop a shared understanding.

3. Identify duplicates and remove.

4. Organize the sticky notes into groupings that make sense.

5. Identify the umbrella focus that captures your vision/focus/purpose. Consider questions such as "What kind of learning do we want for our students?"

6. Identify two or three goals to attain the identified focus.

7. Review the current initiatives/programs. Do not try to make them all fit the new focus. Select only the ones that support the core goals and place them under the goals.

8. Review the list of initiatives/programs to eliminate those that are not high impact. You may want to rate each one's impact on a scale of 1 to 5, with 5 having the most impact on student learning.

9. Develop a strategy that supports each goal.

10. Place the other sticky notes aside and determine whether they are essential to support the goals, should be stopped, or should be listed as maintenance structures or processes.

Vision/Focus/Purpose		
Goal 1	**Goal 2**	**Goal 3**
Strategies	**Strategies**	**Strategies**

8. Reduce, Reframe, Remove
Protocol (Continued)

Part B: Reframe

1. Develop a diagram that makes the focus, goals, and support strategy clear for everyone. For an example, see the Accelerated Learning Model for Park Manor School on page 104 in *Coherence*.

2. Make the connections explicit and integrated.

3. Recognize that those who participated in the Reduce phase have a clear picture of how the parts are connected. Find ways for those not engaged in the initial process to have the same dialogue about what the pieces mean and how they relate to their roles.

4. Communicate the messages broadly. Use a variety of methods to communicate, such as social media, focus groups, presentations, and print. Ensure staff have multiple opportunities to engage in conversations about the messages.

Part C: Remove

1. Ask a question, such as "What takes our time and attention away from achieving our focus of improved student learning?"

2. Use brainstorming techniques, such as the sticky notes, to identify time wasters and inefficiencies.

3. Organize the distractors into categories, such as bureaucracy/administration, competing priorities, and so on.

4. Form multi-role task teams to tackle each category and recommend changes (e.g., how to reduce paperwork by 25%).

5. Use the process to give leaders permission to say "no" to the multitude of requests that bombard schools and districts if they do not fit with the focus and goals.

6. Use the focus and goals as criteria for adding any new priorities or demands. Ask, "How will this new initiative, requirement, or task support the focus, goals, and strategy?"

9. Change Quality Quadrant Protocol

Purpose

- Apply the Change Quality Quadrant Protocol to assess the school/district change processes.

Link

Reading: Pages 24–27 from *Coherence: The Right Drivers in Action for Schools, Districts, and Systems,* by Michael Fullan and Joanne Quinn (Corwin, 2015).

"Successful change processes are a function of shaping and reshaping good ideas as they build capacity and ownership" (page 25). Clarity about goals is not sufficient; leaders must develop shared understanding in people's minds and collective action. Coherence becomes a function of the interplay between the growing *explicitness of the strategy* and the *quality of the change culture.* The two variables—explicitness of the strategy and quality of the change culture—interact to create four different results.

Change Quality Quadrant Protocol

The Change Quality Quadrant Protocol displays the relationship between the culture of an organization and the explicitness of the change strategy. Each quadrant describes the degree to which a culture supports change.

1. Brainstorm as a team all the changes you are implementing in your school or district and place each idea on a sticky note.

2. Assess each change initiative and consider evidence of explicitness of the strategy and the strength of the culture for each initiative. Mark the sticky note as belonging to quadrant 1, 2, 3, or 4. Post on chart paper or wall.

3. For each change initiative, discuss the following:

   - What is effective/ineffective about the explicitness of the strategy?
   - What is effective/ineffective about the culture for change?
   - How can we increase the explicitness of the strategy or enhance the quality of the change culture so it moves to quadrant 4?

Change Quality Quadrant

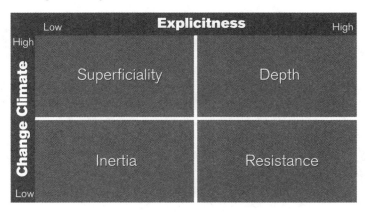

Change Climate (vertical axis):

Describes the degree to which a culture supports change by fostering trust, nonjudgmentalism, leadership, innovation, and collaboration

Explicitness (horizontal axis):

Describes the degree of explicitness of the strategy, including precision of the goals, clarity of the strategy, use of data, and supports

Source: Graphic by Taryn Hauritz.

10. Carousel Brainstorming Protocol

Purpose

- Examine the change processes needed to help people change their practices.
- Identify strategies to support people at each stage of the change process.

Link

Reading: Pages 27–29 from *Coherence: The Right Drivers in Action for Schools, Districts, and Systems,* by Michael Fullan and Joanne Quinn (Corwin, 2015).

Change is a process, not an event. The role of the leader is to manage the transition from the current state to the future state and to create the culture and supports that provide the confidence and competence needed for people to try new behaviors and practices.

The metaphor of two fishbowls describes the challenge of supporting individuals and organizations to move from current to future practice.

Shifting Practice

Familiar

As we consider the bowl on the left, most fish feel comfortable in their bowl because they are familiar with their circumstances, even though they may be dissatisfied.

The expectations of the kind of swimming are traditional and known.

The level of collaboration is the status quo—they know who is in the bowl and how to interact.

The current rewards are understood, and they know how to survive.

Unknown

Contrast that with the bowl on the right, which is full of unknowns.

The expectations of the kind of leaping and swimming required in the new bowl are unclear.

Collaboration is not yet established, so they have few friends or colleagues and the support structures are unknown.

Rewards are distant and often lack specificity while the dangers of leaping are in the present.

Source: Graphic by Taryn Hauritz.

10. Carousel Brainstorming Protocol (Continued)

The Carousel Brainstorming Protocol activates prior knowledge and uses collaborative discussion and movement to generate new thinking or solve problems.

1. Create three charts with the numbers 1 to 3 and one topic at the top of each chart. See an example below. Post the charts in sequence on the walls around the meeting room.

2. Divide into three teams and assign each team to a chart. Ensure each team has a different colored marker so it is easy to see who generated the ideas if questions arise.

3. Teams have 3 minutes to generate and record strategies for their topic; for example, what strategies will build the capacity of teachers to "leap" (try new practices)?

4. After 3 minutes, teams move to the next chart. Teams should read what has been created and then clarify, extend, or add new ideas. Repeat at 3-minute intervals until all charts have been visited.

5. Teams should review their final chart, synthesize and evaluate the ideas, and select 3–5 of the best strategies to share with the large group.

6. Discuss in the large group and select the most promising strategies for action.

1. Conditions That Support Teachers' "Leap"	2. Strategies to Recognize Early "Leaping" Innovators	3. Strategies to Build Capacity

11. Turn and Talk Protocol

Purpose

- Link the push and pull factors to personal leadership strategies.

Links

Video: "Topic Series 19: The Push and Pull Factor," available at http://www.michaelfullan.ca/topic-video-the-push-pull-factor

Reading: Pages 33–34 from *Coherence: The Right Drivers in Action for Schools, Districts, and Systems,* by Michael Fullan and Joanne Quinn (Corwin, 2015).

A good leader has high expectations for the system, but this can't be imposed—buy-in is required. The *push* part of leadership is to make sure the high expectation is there; the *pull* part of leadership combines intrinsic motivation and people wanting to work together with a high moral imperative and a path to get there.

If you combine push and pull, you can accomplish a lot in a short period of time.

Turn and Talk Protocol

The Turn and Talk Protocol builds reflection skills and develops conversations between colleagues to share experiences and ideas.

After reading or viewing "The Push and Pull Factor," reflect on a time when you may have been too "pushy" or too "pully." Share the example with a partner.

12. Think-Pair-Share Protocol

Purpose

- Examine push and pull strategies in action.
- Reflect on the use of push and pull strategies in leadership roles at the school or district.

Link

Video: "Our Teamwork Approach: Peters K–3 Elementary," available at http://www.michaelfullan.ca/our-teamwork-approach-peters-k-3-elementary

Think-Pair-Share Protocol

This cooperative group strategy encourages pairs to reflect on a particular topic and then discuss. It ensures full participation and encourages deep dialogue when prompted by a video.

1. Form pairs to view the video "Our Teamwork Approach: Peters K–3 Elementary." Designate one partner to look for examples of "push" strategies and one to look for examples of "pull" strategies.

2. After viewing, partners share their examples of push and pull strategies.

3. In a large group, discuss ways the leader integrated push and pull strategies.

13. Both Sides Now Protocol

Purpose

- Develop integrated strategy using the concepts of push and pull.

Both Sides Now Protocol

The Both Sides Now Protocol is an opportunity to examine a strategy by brainstorming the positive and negative implications of the strategy. Participants then make judgments about the best possible strategy.

1. Think of a change leadership issue you are facing. Identify the push and pull strategies you might use. Record them in the middle column of the Both Sides Now Organizer.

2. Analyze the potential implications—positive and negative—of each strategy and record them in the Both Sides Now Organizer.

3. Select a course of action that combines push and pull strategies that will be optimal for the issue in question.

Both Sides Now Organizer

Positive Implications	Potential Push Strategies	Negative Implications

Positive Implications	Potential Pull Strategies	Negative Implications

14. Integration Inventory Protocol

Purpose

- Examine the degree of vertical and horizontal integration in the school or district.
- Identify strategies to foster greater vertical or horizontal integration.

Link

Reading: Pages 34–35 from *Coherence: The Right Drivers in Action for Schools, Districts, and Systems,* by Michael Fullan and Joanne Quinn (Corwin, 2015).

"Change leaders are intentional in developing relationships, shared understanding, and mutual accountability vertically (at every level of the organization) and horizontally (across schools, departments, and divisions). The catalyst is mobilizing meaningful joint work and learning from that work. As groups go deeper into solution finding, they become clearer about purpose and strengthen commitment to the goals. Focused vertical and lateral interaction over time fosters greater shared coherence" (page 34).

Integration Inventory Protocol

This protocol examines the vertical and horizontal degree of integration at the school and district levels.

1. Use the following inventory with your leadership team to analyze the patterns of integration that exist vertically and horizontally in your school and district.

2. Identify the structures and processes currently used to link purpose and practices. Identify evidence that the structure or process is effective.

3. Have peers place colored dots on each cell to indicate the effectiveness of the current processes. Peers should do this simultaneously to avoid groupthink.

   - red: no implementation
   - yellow: early stages of implementation
   - green: effective implementation

4. Discuss and record areas of strength. How can these be maintained?

5. Discuss and record gaps or areas of need. What is not being addressed? What needs to be increased or enhanced?

14. Integration Inventory Protocol (Continued)

Change Leadership—Capacity and Integration

Schools

Vertical Integration Across Grades/Departments	Evidence
• Purpose and goals	
• Structures and processes for deep collaboration	
• Precision in pedagogy	
• Accountability measures	
Horizontal Integration Between Grade Levels and Administration	**Evidence**
• Purpose and goals	
• Structures and processes for deep collaboration	
• Precision in pedagogy	
• Accountability measures	

(Continued)

(Continued)

Districts

Vertical Integration Between Districts and Schools	Evidence
• Purpose and goals	
• Structures and processes for deep collaboration	
• Precision in pedagogy	
• Accountability measures	

Horizontal Integration Across Schools	Evidence
• Purpose and goals	
• Structures and processes for deep collaboration	
• Precision in pedagogy	
• Accountability measures	

Change Leadership— Capacity and Integration

Chapter 3

Cultivating Collaborative Cultures

15. Concept Attainment Protocol   27

16. Video Viewing Advance Organizer Protocol   28

17. Four A's Protocol   30

18. Lead Learner Competencies Protocol   31

19. Reciprocal Teaching Protocol   32

20. Sticky Note Clustering Protocol   34

21. Read, Record, Retell, Relate, and Reflect Protocol   36

15. Concept Attainment Protocol

Purpose

- Develop an understanding of the growth mind-set.

Link

Reading: Pages 49–53 from *Coherence: The Right Drivers in Action for Schools, Districts, and Systems,* by Michael Fullan and Joanne Quinn (Corwin, 2015).

Concept Attainment Protocol

The Concept Attainment Protocol is an inductive thinking strategy that develops concepts by exploring "yes" examples, which have the characteristics of the concepts, and "no" examples, which do not have the characteristics. Using these examples, the big ideas, the concepts are developed (Bruner, Goodnow, & Austin, 1967).

1. Review each of the statements below.

2. Decide whether the statement reflects a growth mind-set or not.

3. Share with a colleague and provide a rationale for your decisions.

4. Develop a definition of a "growth mind-set."

Yes?		No?
	The district that selects leaders from a pool of volunteers, puts them through a rigorous competition process, and places them in an environment of competition and a win-at-all-costs mentality provides stronger leadership.	
	People have an innate desire to belong and contribute.	
	When developing a school or district plan, it is better to seek the advice of external consultants.	
	Collaboration is powerful but takes too much time when solutions are needed quickly.	
	To meet the curriculum requirements, it is more productive to purchase programs.	
	Blending sustained capacity building with a reliance on talent from within leads to stronger student performance.	

··

16. Video Viewing Advance Organizer Protocol

··

Purpose

- Apply growth mind-set knowledge.
- Assess learning leadership qualities.

Link

Video: "Our Digital Journey: William G. Davis Sr. Public School," available at http://www.michael fullan.ca/ontario-wg-davis

"Creating a culture of growth is a start, but leaders need to intentionally orchestrate the work of teachers, leaders, and peers and keep it focused on collaboratively improving student learning" (page 53).

Video Viewing Advance Organizer Protocol

The Video Viewing Advance Organizer Protocol provides a focus for viewing and fosters both reflection and dialogue.

1. View the video "Our Digital Journey: William G. Davis Sr. Public School" and record evidence of "learning leadership" on the advance organizer.

2. Form a group of four and share the evidence for each component.

16. Video Viewing Advance Organizer Protocol (Continued)

Competencies	Evidence
Modeling learning	
Shaping culture	
Maximizing impact on learning	

Learning Leadership

17. Four A's Protocol

Purpose

- Reflect on the leadership qualities of the principal or leader.

Four A's Protocol

The Four A's Protocol helps readers or viewers make sense of the content by thinking about their assumptions, agreements, arguments, and actions (Gray, 2005).

After viewing the video "Our Digital Journey: William G. Davis Sr. Public School," complete the Four A's Chart to summarize the lead learner's actions.

Four A's Chart

Assumptions	Agreements
What assumptions can you make about the work the principal had done prior to the video?	What competencies did the principal display as a lead learner?
Arguments	**Actions**
Was there anything you would have done differently?	What are the next steps for the principal as lead learner?

18. Lead Learner Competencies Protocol

Purpose

- Assess the attributes of Lead Learner Competencies and identify areas of growth.

Lead Learner Competencies Protocol

This protocol allows individuals to reflect on strengths by citing evidence and then identify areas for growth.

Complete this chart individually and reflect on your strengths and areas for growth.

Competencies	Criteria	Evidence
Modeling learning	• Participate as a learner • Lead capacity building • Make learning a priority • Foster leadership at all levels	
Shaping culture	• Build relational trust and relationships • Create structures and process for collaborative work • Support cycles of learning and application • Engage others in solving complex problems • Resource strategically	
Maximizing learning	• Focus on precision in learning and teaching • Establish a small number of goals • Create a clear strategy for achieving goals • Orchestrate the work of coaches, teacher leaders, and support personnel around student learning • Monitor impact on learning through collaborative inquiry	

Learning Leadership

19. Reciprocal Teaching Protocol

Purpose

- Deepen understanding of capacity building.

Link

Reading: Pages 56–60 from *Coherence: The Right Drivers in Action for Schools, Districts, and Systems,* by Michael Fullan and Joanne Quinn (Corwin, 2015).

"Capacity building is a key lever for developing coherence because as knowledge and skills are being developed, the collaborative culture is deepened, shared meaning is clarified, and commitment is reinforced" (page 56).

Reciprocal Teaching Protocol

This protocol encourages the skills of predicting, reading, summarizing, questioning, and clarifying to ensure understanding of content (Palincsar & Brown, 1984).

1. Form a trio.

2. Prior to reading the section "Capacity Building" (pages 56–60), make predictions about the content of the excerpt.

3. Record your responses to the reciprocal teaching prompts on the advance organizer.

4. Following the reading, raise questions connected to capacity building.

5. Clarify the questions.

6. Describe the power of capacity building.

19. Reciprocal Teaching Protocol (Continued)

Predict the content.
Read and summarize.
Ask questions about capacity building.
Clarify the content.
Describe the most powerful aspects of capacity building.

Capacity Building Criteria and Impact

20. Sticky Note Clustering Protocol

Purpose

- Review protocols for meaningful collaboration.
- Reflect and plan for deeper strategies for collaborative learning.

Link

Reading: Pages 60–64 from *Coherence: The Right Drivers in Action for Schools, Districts, and Systems,* by Michael Fullan and Joanne Quinn (Corwin, 2015).

Sticky Note Clustering Protocol

This protocol enables individuals to first reflect on a topic and then to organize thinking into bigger ideas. As a group contributes ideas, new concepts can be formed and explored (Bruner et al., 1967).

1. List all the capacity building/professional learning initiatives or programs that are in your school currently, and write the name of each initiative or program on a separate sticky note.

2. Assess each sticky note to determine the depth of the learning design and the degree of collaboration.

3. Place the sticky notes on the Shifting Organizational Practice grid.

4. Consider the following:

   - What are the most promising approaches?
   - What might you do to make some approaches more effective?

Shifting Organizational Practice

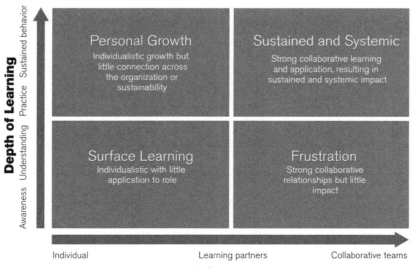

Source: Graphic by Taryn Hauritz.

20. Sticky Note Clustering Protocol (Continued)

Personal Growth	Sustained and Systemic
Activities that focus on individual growth.	Strong collaborative learning and application, resulting in sustained and systemic impact.

Surface Learning	Frustration
Individualistic with little application to role.	Strong collaborative relationships but with little impact.

....

21. Read, Record, Retell, Relate, and Reflect Protocol

....

Purpose

- Review protocols for meaningful collaboration.

Link

Reading: Pages 64–73 from *Coherence: The Right Drivers in Action for Schools, Districts, and Systems,* by Michael Fullan and Joanne Quinn (Corwin, 2015).

The Five R's Protocol

The Five R's Protocol ensures understanding of content by reading, recording, and then retelling. The next steps for deeper learning are to connect to previous experiences and to reflect on both the content and application.

1. Form a group of three.

   - Person 1 reads "Collaborative Inquiry" (pages 64–67).
   - Person 2 reads "Networks" (pages 68–70).
   - Person 3 reads "Harnessing the Power of Personal Learning Networks 2.0" (pages 70–73).

2. Teach your reading to your group of three. Record notes in the Record and Retell column of the Five R's Protocol organizer.

3. As a team, relate the reading to your experiences.

4. Reflect and record ideas for going deeper with each of the collaborative practices.

21. Read, Record, Retell, Relate, and Reflect Protocol (Continued)

Read	Record and Retell	Relate to Your Experiences	Reflect on Going Deeper With Strategies
Collaborative Inquiry			
Networks			
Personal Learning Networks			

Chapter 4

Deepening Learning

22. Affinity Protocol   39

23. 6Cs Protocol   40

24. Through the Looking Glass Protocol   43

25. Shifting Instructional Practices Protocol   45

26. Instructional Coherence Framework Protocol   47

22. Affinity Protocol

Purpose

- Examine a process for clarifying learning goals.

Link

Video: Select videos on problem-based, project-based, or inquiry learning from sites including the following:

Edutopia (www.edutopia.org)
EL Education (www.eleducation.org)
Teaching Channel (www.teachingchannel.org)

Affinity Protocol

The Affinity Protocol is a cooperative structure that fosters participation by requiring individual contribution to the discussion. It brings out a variety of perspectives on a common issue or problem and uses deep dialogue to assist the group to explore similarities and differences and then reach consensus.

1. Share a video that stimulates peers to think about what might be possible for students in the global, digital world (e.g., "Rubik's Cube: A Question, Waiting to Be Answered," available on YouTube).

2. Use turn and talk to have peers discuss what excited them about the video and the type of learning that they saw.

3. Ask peers to think about a young person they know and care about. As they think about that young person, they should consider the question, "What do you want students to know, be able to do, and be like when they leave school?"

4. Generate individually 6–8 attributes/qualities/descriptors and place one idea on each of 6–8 sticky notes.

5. Form groups of four to six and provide chart paper. Group members place all the sticky notes on the chart in any order.

6. Read all the sticky notes and begin to create groupings of similar ideas. The key at this stage is to have a deep dialogue about the meaning behind the words on the sticky notes, to find areas of agreement.

7. Label each category.

8. Charts can be posted for a gallery walk. Ask peers to look for similarities and themes that emerge across the different charts.

9. Synthesize the charts to create one list that captures the key learning goals for the group.

Clarity of Learning Goals

· ·

23. 6Cs Protocol

· ·

Purpose

- Build a shared understanding of the 6Cs (deep learning competencies).

Link

Reading: Pages 83–88 from *Coherence: The Right Drivers in Action for Schools, Districts, and Systems,* by Michael Fullan and Joanne Quinn (Corwin, 2015).

The 6Cs

Communication

- Coherent communication using a range of modes
- Communication designed for different audiences
- Substantive, multimodal communication
- Reflection on and use of the process of learning to improve communication

Critical Thinking

- Evaluating information and arguments
- Making connections and identifying patterns
- Problem solving
- Meaningful knowledge construction
- Experimenting, reflecting, and taking action on ideas in the real world

Collaboration

- Working interdependently as a team
- Interpersonal and team-related skills
- Social, emotional, and intercultural skills
- Management of team dynamics and challenges

Creativity

- Economic and social entrepreneurialism
- Asking the right inquiry questions
- Considering and pursuing novel ideas and solutions
- Leadership for action

Character

- Learning to learn
- Grit, tenacity, perseverance, and resilience
- Self-regulation and responsibility
- Empathy for and contributing to the safety and benefit of others

Citizenship

- A global perspective
- Understanding of diverse values and worldviews
- Genuine interest in human and environmental sustainability
- Solving ambiguous, complex, and authentic problems

....

23. 6Cs Protocol (Continued)

....

Deep Learning Competencies—6Cs Protocol

The 6Cs Protocol provides an advance organizer for thinking about deep learning competencies as identified. The placemat organizer can be used to activate prior knowledge about the six competencies or to look for examples of the 6Cs using video exemplars (e.g., www.npdl.global).

1. Form groups of six with each peer assigned one of the 6Cs.

2. Review the descriptors of the six deep learning competencies. Each group member is responsible for one competency and provides an example of what that competency might look like and sound like in practice or how it is being developed in his or her classroom or school.

3. Share the examples within the group of six.

4. Select a video of classroom practice and analyze it for examples of how the six deep learning competencies are being developed. Use the same graphic organizer to record evidence.

5. Discuss ways to incorporate one or more of the competencies in future learning designs.

Clarity of Learning Goals

Clarity of Learning Goals

23. 6Cs Protocol (Continued)

Communication	Creativity
Critical Thinking	**Character**
Collaboration	**Citizenship**

24. Through the Looking Glass Protocol

Purpose

- Develop common language and practice to increase precision in pedagogy.
- Use a simulation for examining classroom practices.

Links

Video: Select videos of classroom practice that model the instructional strategies you want to increase or enhance in your school or district. Good sources include the following:

Edutopia (www.edutopia.org)
EL Education (www.eleducation.org)
Teaching Channel (www.teachingchannel.org)

Reading: Pages 88–99 from *Coherence: The Right Drivers in Action for Schools, Districts, and Systems,* by Michael Fullan and Joanne Quinn (Corwin, 2015).

Through the Looking Glass Protocol

This protocol enables analysis of classroom or school practices. The advance organizer placemat targets the focus of the analysis and provides a vehicle for building shared knowledge and understanding while increasing individual and collective responsibility.

1. Select a video for viewing and provide the advance organizer placemat. Assign the purpose for viewing. Peers may work in a trio with each member watching for evidence of one element, or each peer may view and record evidence of all elements.

2. Discuss the evidence in small groups. Consider discussion questions such as the following:

   - What strategies were most effective? Why?
   - What did the teacher need to know or do prior to this learning experience?
   - What experiences did students likely have prior to this experience that prepared them for success?
   - What strategies are we already using in our practice?
   - What strategies would we like to use more often or add?
   - How are we increasing precision in pedagogy in the school or district?
   - How might we increase precision in the next month?

3. Examine the three strands that comprise the new pedagogies needed to foster deep learning competencies.

   - Pedagogical partnerships
   - Learning environments
   - Leveraging digital

Precision in Pedagogy

....

24. Through the Looking
Glass Protocol (Continued)

....

4. Record evidence of the pedagogy as you view each video.

New Pedagogy	Evidence
Pedagogical partnerships Pedagogical practices that engage students in codesigning authentic, relevant learning	
Learning environments Creation of conditions that foster risk taking, build on student interests and strengths, and develop collaborative learning	
Leveraging digital Integration of digital that accelerates and deepens learning	

25. Shifting Instructional Practices Protocol

Purpose

- Analyze the strategies used to create a culture that shifts instructional practice.

Links

Video: "Our Journey to Awesome: Park Manor Public School," available at http://www.michael fullan.ca/ontario-park-manor

Reading: Pages 99–105 from *Coherence: The Right Drivers in Action for Schools, Districts, and Systems,* by Michael Fullan and Joanne Quinn (Corwin, 2015).

Shifting Instructional Practices Protocol

This protocol focuses the viewing of a video by using a jigsaw structure to increase accountability and foster deeper dialogue. The protocol can be used while viewing a school or district case to analyze conditions and actions that shift practices.

1. Prepare for viewing by reviewing the four conditions needed to change teaching practices across the school or district.

2. Form groups of four and assign each peer one dimension of the organizer to observe critically while viewing.

3. After viewing, peers share the evidence they recorded about each of the four dimensions.

4. Discuss as a group:

    - What actions or approaches were most important in improving this school?
    - What actions of the principal were most crucial?
    - What are you doing in your school that is similar?
    - What actions might you consider as a result of this viewing?
    - What support could district leaders provide to support this work?

Precision in Pedagogy

25. Shifting Instructional Practices Protocol (Continued)

Dimension	Observations
Vision and goals	
Leadership for deep learning	
Creating a culture for learning	
Leveraging digital	

26. Instructional Coherence Framework Protocol

Purpose

- Analyze the strategies used to create a culture that shifts instructional practice.

Links

Video: "Our Journey to Awesome: Park Manor Public School" available at http://www.michaelfullan.ca/ontario-park-manor

Reading: Pages 99–105 from *Coherence: The Right Drivers in Action for Schools, Districts, and Systems,* by Michael Fullan and Joanne Quinn (Corwin, 2015).

Instructional Coherence Framework Protocol

This protocol stimulates the development of a visual summary of the key components of a school's or district's instructional process. It builds common language and clarity of strategy through the collaborative design process.

Part A: Analyzing an Instructional Coherence Framework

1. Form pairs to review the Accelerated Learning Model that was viewed in the "Our Journey to Awesome" video (page 104).

2. Pose questions such as the following:

   - What do you like about the framework?
   - What questions do you have about the framework?
   - How might a framework be useful in your role?
   - What are you using currently to describe your instructional focus?
   - How well are the instructional priorities of your school or district understood by everyone?
   - What degree of common language is used to describe the priorities?
   - What common instructional practices are identified in your school or district?
   - To what degree are instructional practices used consistently by all educators?
   - How well are the instructional practices communicated to students and families?

Precision in Pedagogy

....

26. Instructional Coherence
Framework Protocol (Continued)

....

Part B: Designing an
Instructional Coherence Framework Protocol

1. Brainstorm a list of your instructional priorities and a list of the instructional practices/strategies you expect to be used in your school or district.

2. Create a visual that integrates these elements and communicates to a wide audience of users.

3. Determine how you will simulate this process with others to build understanding and ownership.

Chapter 5

Securing Accountability

27. Three-Step Interview Protocol   50

··

27. Three-Step Interview Protocol

··

Purpose

- Know the power of both internal and external accountability.
- Understand the importance of securing internal accountability through capacity building.
- Develop strategies to incorporate external accountability.

Link

Reading: Excerpts below from Chapter 5 of *Coherence: The Right Drivers in Action for Schools, Districts, and Systems,* by Michael Fullan and Joanne Quinn (Corwin, 2015).

Securing Accountability

"The argument is this: If you want effective accountability, you need to develop conditions that maximize *internal accountability*—conditions that increase the likelihood that people will be accountable to themselves and to the group. Second, you need to frame and reinforce internal accountability with *external accountability*—standards, expectations, transparent data, and selective interventions" (page 109).

Internal Accountability

"Simply stated, accountability is taking responsibility for one's actions. At the core of accountability in educational systems is student learning. As City, Elmore, Fiarman, and Teitel (2009) argue, 'the real accountability system is in the tasks that students are asked to do' (p. 23). Constantly improving and refining instructional practice so that students can engage in deep learning tasks is perhaps the single most important responsibility of the teaching profession and educational systems as a whole. In this sense, accountability as defined here is not limited to mere gains in test scores but on deeper and more meaningful learning for all students.

"Internal accountability occurs when individuals and groups willingly take on personal, professional, and collective responsibility for continuous improvement and success for all students (Hargreaves & Shirley, 2009)" (page 110).

External Accountability

"External accountability is when system leaders reassure the public through transparency, monitoring, and selective intervention that their system is performing in line with societal expectations and requirements. The priority for policy makers, we argue, should be to lead with creating the conditions for internal accountability because they are more effective in achieving greater overall accountability, including external accountability. Policy makers also have direct responsibilities to address external accountability, but this latter function will be far more effective if they get the internal part right" (page 111).

(Continued)

(Continued)

Role of the System

"With strong internal accountability as the context, the external accountability role of the system includes the following:

1. Establishing and promoting professional standards and practices, including performance appraisal, undertaken by professionally respected peers and leaders in teams wherever possible, and developing the expertise of teachers and teacher-leaders so that they can undertake these responsibilities. With the robust judgments of respected leaders and peers, getting rid of teachers and administrators who should not be in the profession will become a transparent collective responsibility.

2. Ongoing monitoring of the performance of the system, including direct intervention with schools and districts in cases of persistent underperformance.

3. Insisting on reciprocal accountability that manages 'up' as well as down so that systems are held accountable for providing the resources and supports that are essential to enable schools and teachers to fulfill expectations (e.g., 'failing' schools should not be closed when they have been insufficiently resourced; individual teachers should be evaluated in the context of whether they have been forced into different grade assignments every year or have experienced constant leadership instability).

4. Adopting and applying indicators of organizational health as a context for individual teacher and leader performance, such as staff retention rates, leadership turnover rates, teacher absenteeism levels, numbers of crisis-related incidents, and so on, in addition to outcome indicators of student performance and well-being. These would include measures of social capital in the teaching profession such as extent of collaboration and levels of collegial trust. Outcome measures for students should also, as previously stated, include multiple measures, including well-being, students' sense of control over their own destiny (locus of control), levels of engagement in learning, and so forth" (page 120).

Internal and External Accountability

Internal and External Accountability

27. Three-Step Interview Protocol (Continued)

Three-Step Interview Protocol

The Three-Step Interview Protocol engages three partners in discussion on a particular topic using focused questions (Kagan, 1989).

Through a rotation as depicted below, each participate experiences the three roles: recorder, interviewer, and respondent. This ensures accountability for active involvement and for effective listening.

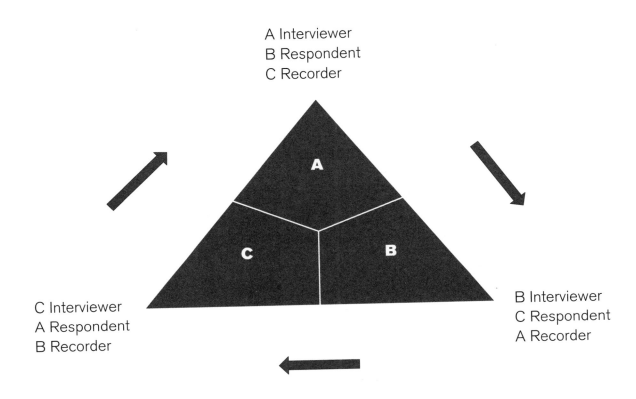

A Interviewer
B Respondent
C Recorder

C Interviewer
A Respondent
B Recorder

B Interviewer
C Respondent
A Recorder

Source: Adapted from Kagan (1989).

1. Form teams of three and designate persons A, B, and C.

2. Read independently the content provided and then think about responses to the questions.

3. Begin the cycle with person A as the interviewer, B as the respondent, and C as the recorder, using the advance organizer.

4. Provide 4 minutes for the respondent to be interviewed and then switch positions. Continue the cycle until all participants have been interviewed.

27. Three-Step Interview Protocol (Continued)

Question	Person A	Person B	Person C
1. How would you distinguish between internal and external accountability?			
2. Describe strategies your school/district uses to build internal accountability.			
3. What steps will you take to ensure the effective implementation of external accountability?			

Chapter 6

Leading for Coherence

28. Check for Understanding Protocol   55

29. Reviewing Leadership Plan Protocol: Part A   57

30. Reviewing Leadership Plan Protocol: Part B   58

··

28. Check for Understanding Protocol

··

Purpose

- Understand the importance of developing leaders at all levels.

Links

Video: "Topic Series 7: Leadership at All Levels," available at http://www.michaelfullan.ca/topic-video-leadership-at-all-levels

Reading: Pages 134–135 from *Coherence: The Right Drivers in Action for Schools, Districts, and Systems,* by Michael Fullan and Joanne Quinn (Corwin, 2015).

Check for Understanding Protocol

This protocol asks participants to read a passage and summarize the main ideas in a short paragraph. Then, with a partner, the summaries are shared and reviewed to check for understanding of the main ideas.

1. View the video.

2. Read the passage above from the book.

3. Prepare a short summary of the main ideas of the passage.

4. With a partner, share each summary.

5. Record on the advance organizer similarities and differences between the two summaries.

6. As a pair, decide on the three most important ideas gleaned from the passage.

28. Check for Understanding Protocol (Continued)

Your Summary of the Passage	

Comparing Summaries	
Similarities	**Differences**

Three Main Ideas
1.
2.
3.

29. Reviewing Leadership Plan Protocol: Part A

Purpose

- Identify current professional learning for formal and informal leaders in the school or district.
- Plan for developing leaders at all levels.

Link

Reading: Chapter 3, Protocol 18: Lead Learner Competencies; pages 54–60 from *Coherence: The Right Drivers in Action for Schools, Districts, and Systems,* by Michael Fullan and Joanne Quinn (Corwin, 2015).

Part A: Reviewing Your Current Leadership Development Plan Protocol

This protocol engages school- or district-level teams in reflection on the professional learning provided for both formal and informal leaders.

1. Use the advance organizer to record the structures, processes, and professional learning currently in place to develop formal and informal leaders.

2. Discuss strengths and note gaps and areas for improvement.

Leadership Development Plan

Formal Leaders	New Leaders	Aspiring Leaders	Informal Leaders

Developing Leaders

30. Reviewing Leadership Plan Protocol: Part B

Part B: Professional Learning for Formal and Informal Leaders Protocol

A protocol for professional learning for both formal and informal leaders helps to develop a consistent and coherent vision of the school or district for the future. It will reinforce beliefs about the value and roles of effective leaders and identify potential leaders. Professional learning will promote a common understanding and language of the district's core values and goals as well as assist with achieving the goals.

The strategy should be based on the principles of adult learning and provide an opportunity for leaders to help design, facilitate, and participate in a variety of new learning experiences.

a. Develop at least two strategies to support leadership in your district and record them on the advance organizer.

b. Prompts for professional leadership development plan:

- **Formal leaders:** how do you connect leaders to discuss current issues, learn new skills and competencies, be part of the district planning, help others grow?
- **New leaders:** how do you support leaders in their new roles? What support do you provide for leaders to deepen their skills and competencies? How do new leaders learn about the district and its expectations, values, goals, and strategies to achieve goals?
- **Aspiring leaders:** how do you select and encourage new leaders? What do you do to develop their knowledge, skills, and behaviors to help them become an effective leader? What opportunities do you provide for leadership experiences? Do your selection criteria and process support use multiple sources of evidence to demonstrate leadership potential?
- **Informal leaders:** how do you encourage informal leadership, such as teacher leaders? What support do you provide to assist informal leaders?

c. Think about who will be involved in the identification of content, processes, organization, and facilitation. How will you monitor the success of the learning experiences?

30. Reviewing Leadership
Plan Protocol: Part B (Continued)

Strategies	Who will be involved?	What will you provide?	How will you measure success?
Formal Leaders 1. 2. 3.			
New Leaders 1. 2. 3.			
Aspiring Leaders 1. 2. 3.			
Informal Leaders 1. 2. 3.			

Chapter 7

Mastering the Framework

31. Taking Action Protocol   61

32. Coherence Progression Protocol   63

33. Coherence Planning Protocol   73

31. Taking Action Protocol

Purpose

- Identify key actions for the school or district for each component of the coherence framework.

Link

Reading: Key actions in the following Taking Action Protocol and the infographics at the conclusion of each chapter in *Coherence: The Right Drivers in Action for Schools, Districts, and Systems,* by Michael Fullan and Joanne Quinn (Corwin, 2015).

Taking Action Protocol

The Taking Action Protocol engages leaders and teams in examining their practice on a particular topic using focused questions.

1. Review the key actions provided for each chapter.

2. Record your analysis and decisions for each action step as you complete each chapter, using the advance organizer.

3. Review the collective thinking of the team about each of the action steps after completing Chapter 6. Use this information to guide the next phase using the Coherence Progression Protocol.

Synthesizing Actions for Each Chapter

31. Taking Action Protocol (Continued)

Chapter	Key Actions
1. Coherence Making	1. Develop a strategy for change using the right drivers. 2. Design a process to ensure your goals are clear and understood by all.
2. Focusing Direction	1. Identify the steps you will take to tackle overload, fragmentation, and distractors. 2. Determine a change strategy to support a shift in practice.
3. Cultivating Collaborative Cultures	1. Design a plan to ensure professional learning is sustained and systematic. 2. Develop a plan to strengthen collaborative work.
4. Deepening Learning	1. Design an instructional coherence framework and strategy for implementation.
5. Securing Accountability	1. Identify the strategies you will use to build internal accountability. 2. Outline a plan to ensure effective external accountability.
6. Leading for Coherence	1. Strategize your plan to develop leaders at all levels.

32. Coherence Progression Protocol

Purpose

- Assess the current level of coherence in the school or district using the Coherence Progression Protocol.

Link

Reading: Key actions in the Taking Action Protocol and the infographics at the conclusion of each chapter in *Coherence: The Right Drivers in Action for Schools, Districts, and Systems,* by Michael Fullan and Joanne Quinn (Corwin, 2015).

Coherence Progression Protocol

The Coherence Progression is a protocol for analyzing the current level of coherence for each component of the coherence framework. Use of evidence to justify placement on the progressions focuses deep discussion. Results are synthesized to identify strengths and gaps as well as identify strategies for improvement.

1. Review individually the Coherence Progression and highlight the descriptors that best capture the current level of coherence in the organization.

2. Share and compare ratings across the team. Discuss the rationale for individual ratings and reach consensus on one rating for each dimension. Highlight that rating to create a visual profile.

3. Review the profile to determine the patterns and areas of greatest strength and areas of greatest need.

4. These data, along with the ideas generated in your key actions organizer, will be used to create a 100-Day Coherence Strategy.

Focusing Direction Assessment Sample With Highlighting

Component	Emerging	Accelerating	Mastering
Shared purpose drives action.	• A stated purpose or focus for the organization exists in formal documents but is not widely shared and does not drive decisions.	• The stated purpose and focus are clearly articulated formally, and groups are beginning to articulate this focus in their work. The purpose and focus are beginning to drive decisions but not consistently.	• The purpose and focus are clearly articulated and shared by all levels of the organization. There is strong commitment to the purpose, and it drives decisions at all levels of the school or district.
A small number of goals tied to student learning drives decisions.	• A small number of goals are stated but may be unclear, and there are a number of competing priorities.	• A small number of goals are stated and understood by some, but deep understanding and action is inconsistent across the school or district.	• A small number of goals clearly focused on improving learning are well articulated and implemented by leaders, teachers, and staff at all levels of the system.

Assessing Coherence

32. Coherence Progression Protocol (Continued)

Focusing Direction

Component	Emerging	Accelerating	Mastering
Shared purpose drives action.	• A stated purpose or focus for the organization exists in formal documents but is not widely shared and does not drive decisions.	• The stated purpose and focus are clearly articulated formally, and groups are beginning to articulate this focus in their work. The purpose and focus are beginning to drive decisions but not consistently.	• The purpose and focus are clearly articulated and shared by all levels of the organization. There is strong commitment to the purpose and it drives decisions at all levels of the school or district.
A small number of goals tied to student learning drives decisions.	• A small number of goals are stated but may be unclear, and there are a number of competing priorities. • The school or district may be feeling overload from too many initiatives or priorities. Fragmentation may be felt when the goals do not seem to be connected in a meaningful way.	• A small number of goals are stated and understood by some, but deep understanding and action is inconsistent across the school or district. • The goals drive some decisions but inconsistently. • There is a strategy to reduce the number of competing priorities and eliminate distractors.	• A small number of goals clearly focused on improving learning are well articulated and implemented by leaders, teachers, and staff at all levels of the system. • Decisions are directly aligned to the stated goals. • A vigilant process is in place to remove distractors, base decisions on data, and remain consistent year to year.
A clear strategy for achieving the goals is known by all.	• The strategy for achieving the goals lacks clarity and precision. A few decision makers understand the strategy but is not widely understood at all levels. • A clear link between decisions on the allocation of resources and the priority goals is not evident.	• The strategy for achieving the priority goals is stated but led by a small number of leaders. • Ongoing opportunities for interaction and engagement with doing the work are needed so that clarity and commitment are developed across the school or district. • Decisions and the allocation of resources are linked to priorities but not consistently.	• The strategy for achieving the goals is well defined and can be clearly articulated by all educators at every level of the school or district. • Leaders recognize that it is more important to learn from doing the work and adjusting strategy than having a lengthy front end process. • Decisions and the allocation of resources are driven by the strategy and goals.

(Continued)

(Continued)

Component	Emerging	Accelerating	Mastering
Change knowledge is used to move the district forward.	• Leaders see their role as managing the change process one interaction at a time. They rely on formal roles and structures. • Collaboration between and among leaders and teachers is limited to formal structures. • Deep trusting relationships are not consistent. • There is an effort to build internal capacity but a reliance on external experts and packaged solutions continues. • There are few or inconsistent structures and processes for building vertical and horizontal relationships and learning across the school or district.	• Leaders are beginning to see their role as developing others and creating structures and processes for interaction. However opportunities to develop new leaders both formal and informal are not always evident. • Collaboration and trust are emerging within groups but are inconsistent across the school or district. • Capacity building is recognized as a lever for change and efforts to build the collective capacity of groups is emerging. • There are some structures and processes in place to foster relationships and learning vertically within schools/districts and horizontally across roles within schools and districts.	• Strong leadership with a bias for action exists at all levels of the school or district. • Leaders are intentionally developed at all levels. • A culture of collaboration with deep trust and risk taking has been fostered at all levels to promote innovation and shifts in practice. • Capacity building is a key lever for building confidence and competence and pervades the culture. • The culture uses the group to change the group by fostering strong vertical and horizontal relationships and learning opportunities.

32. Coherence Progression Protocol (Continued)

Cultivating Collaborative Cultures

Component	Emerging	Accelerating	Mastering
A growth mind-set underlies the culture.	• A comprehensive internal leadership development strategy is not in place. Leaders build their capacity individually through courses, workshops, and conferences and less frequently in collaboration with others. • There is a reliance on experts to "fix" the problem or for prepackaged solutions. • There is a reliance on external hires for leadership and key roles rather than a focus on building internal capacity.	• An intentional strategy for developing internal leadership is emerging. • There is a commitment to move from individual development to collaborative learning. • Talent is being noticed and nurtured, but strategies may not yet be consistent across the entire school or district. • Capacity to lead internally driven solutions is growing. • The reliance on external hires, programs, or experts to "fix" the problem and prepackaged solutions is decreasing.	• Leaders possess a growth mind-set that builds capacity in themselves and others. A comprehensive strategy is in place to develop the next generation of leaders from within. • The organization views problems and challenges as an opportunity to grow capacity. They see internal expertise as the driver of solutions and innovation in policy and practice and have ways to identify and mobilize that talent. • Rich and diverse external resources are use as inputs to their internally driven solution-finding processes.
Leaders model learning themselves and shape a culture of learning.	• Leaders support and send others to learning sessions but rarely participate as learners themselves. • Leaders are beginning to articulate learning as a priority but are unclear or inconsistent with the allocation of resources.	• Leaders participate as lead learners and are beginning to make learning for everyone a priority at the district or school. • Leaders are beginning to identify and develop other leaders at all levels.	• Leaders model learning by participating as learners and by leading robust capacity building in the school or district. • They make learning a priority and actively foster leadership at all levels.

(Continued)

(Continued)

Component	Emerging	Accelerating	Mastering
Leaders model learning themselves and shape a culture of learning. *(Continued)*	• Trust may be developing but is not consistent across the school or district. • The structures and processes that exist, such as PLCs and coaches, may not be well coordinated or targeted to the priorities.	• Leaders are shaping the culture by developing trusting relationships, but these do not exist with all groups. • Structures and processes to support meaningful collaborative work are more common but are inconsistent across the school or district.	• Leaders shape culture by building trust and relationships both vertically and horizontally. • Leaders create structures and processes for collaborative work and support cycles of learning and application. • They provide resources strategically to propel what matters.
Collective capacity building is fostered above individual development.	• Professional learning opportunities exist but often focus on individual needs and are viewed as more of an event than a sustained process. • Inquiry practices are beginning to be used but inconsistently across the school or district. • The level of trust is growing, but there remain some topics that are avoided and an unwillingness to use sharing practices such as peer observation and feedback.	• A culture of learning and collaborative inquiry exists where teachers and leaders reflect on, review, and adjust their teaching and leadership practices. • Learning experiences are designed using effective practices that foster collaboration and application in role. • Trust is growing and practices are becoming more transparent, such as observation and feedback. • These practices are evident but not yet consistent at all levels of the school or district.	• A powerful culture of learning pervades the school or district as "the way we do things here." • Learning collaboratively is the norm. Strong trust exists and supports innovation and risk taking. • Learning opportunities are rich and diverse with an emphasis on collaborative learning. Opportunities to apply the learning in role are supported consistently. • Successes are celebrated and shared and challenges are seen as opportunities for deeper learning.

(Continued)

(Continued)

Component	Emerging	Accelerating	Mastering
Structures and processes support intentional collaborative work.	• There are few resources such as coaches, mentors, or teacher leaders to support implementation. • These supports are not consistently available or focused. • Pockets of collaboration for learning exist, but it is not the norm. • Collaborative practices such as PLCs are not linked to data and use of learning goals for students.	• Structures and processes exist to develop collaborative learning and collective capacity but are inconsistently used across the school or district. • Mechanisms such as coaches, networks, and communities of practice exist but are not yet focused, connected, or consistently used across the school or district.	• Professional learning models include structures and processes to foster collaborative learning that builds collective capacity. • "Learning from the work" involves cycles of application and collaborative inquiry within and across the school and district. • Mechanisms such as coaches, learning networks, and communities of practice consistently support horizontal and vertical development tied to goals.

32. Coherence Progression Protocol (Continued)

Deepening Learning

Component	Emerging	Accelerating	Mastering
Learning goals are clear to everyone and drive instruction.	• The learning goals for students are unclear or conflicting. For example, the relationship between core curriculum standards and deep learning competencies are unspecified. • Some goals to improve precision in pedagogy have been identified but are not clearly articulated or understood. • The strategy for improvement is unclear, implemented inconsistently, or underresourced.	• Learning goals are being articulated, and the link between deep learning competencies and core curriculum standards is being made more visible. • A small number of goals to improve precision in pedagogy is clearly articulated. • A strategy for improvement is clear to leaders but not well understood at all levels or implemented with consistency.	• Learning goals for deep learning competencies and requirements of core curriculum standards are clearly articulated and integrated. • A small number of goals to improve precision in pedagogy is clearly articulated. • A strategy for improvement is clear, well understood, and being implemented consistently and with impact.
A set of effective pedagogical practices are known and used by all educators.	• A comprehensive framework for learning that identifies goals and high-yield pedagogies is in the beginning stages of development but is not understood widely or used consistently to guide learning.	• A comprehensive framework for learning that identifies goals and high-yield pedagogies is articulated but is not yet consistently used across the school or district to design and assess effective learning experiences. • A strategy for fostering deep learning accelerated by digital is being developed.	• A comprehensive framework for learning that identifies goals and high-yield pedagogies is understood by all and used consistently across the school or district to design and assess effective learning experiences. • A clear strategy for fostering deep learning accelerated by digital is being implemented in a culture of trust and risk taking.

(Continued)

Assessing Coherence

Assessing Coherence

(Continued)

Component	Emerging	Accelerating	Mastering
Robust processes such as collaborative inquiry and examining student work are used regularly to improve practice.	• The work of coaches, teacher leaders, and support personnel is left to the local unit and not explicitly tied to the learning goals or priorities. • Deep collaborative practices such as collaborative inquiry and protocols for examining student work may be used by some teachers or some schools, but there is no consistency of practice or support.	• The school or district provides some resources and expertise for collaborative learning structures. • The work of coaches, teacher leaders, and support personnel is coordinated but not consistently across the school or district. • Deep collaborative practices such as collaborative inquiry and protocols for examining student work are being used with greater frequency but inconsistently across the school or district.	• The school or district provides resources and expertise for collaborative learning structures to thrive. • The work of coaches, teacher leaders, and support personnel is well coordinated by the school or district to maximize impact and achieve the student learning goals. • Deep collaborative practices such as collaborative inquiry and protocols for examining student work are used consistently across the school or district. • Collaborative inquiry is used to monitor progress in impacting learning at all levels.

32. Coherence Progression Protocol (Continued)

Securing Accountability

Component	Emerging	Accelerating	Mastering
Educators take responsibility for continuously improving results.	• The school or district is beginning to shift from conditions of control and external accountability to increasing internal accountability by building capacity. • Mechanisms to build precision in pedagogy are beginning but not comprehensive. • Processes such as examination of student work and collaborative inquiry are used by some educators but not consistently in the school or district. • Structures and processes for using data to improve learning are used but not consistently.	• The school or district intentionally develops conditions to increase internal accountability by building capacity. • Mechanisms to build capacity in pedagogy are used frequently but not consistently across the school or district. • Processes such as examination of student work and collaborative inquiry have been introduced but are not used consistently. • Structures and processes for using data to improve learning are in place but not yet used consistently at all levels.	• The school or district develops conditions that maximize internal accountability by building capacity. • Mechanisms to build capacity of precision in pedagogy are comprehensive and used consistently. • Processes such as examination of student work and collaborative inquiry are used to ensure consistency of quality practices across the school or district. • Structures and processes for using data to improve learning are used consistently at all levels and monitored for impact.
Underperformance is an opportunity for growth, not blame.	• Ongoing monitoring of the performance of the system, including direct intervention in cases of persistent underperformance, may be viewed as negative by the system. • Quick fix strategies, such as school closures, terminations, and external prepackaged solutions, are favored.	• Ongoing monitoring of the performance of the system, including direct intervention in cases of persistent underperformance, is viewed as an opportunity for growth. • Interventions such as turnaround schools and performance appraisal systems are developed as a partnership to support improvement.	• Ongoing monitoring of the performance of the system, including direct intervention in cases of persistent underperformance, is an opportunity for growth. • Performance processes are undertaken by respected peers and leaders and developed with teacher leaders so that the quality of teaching becomes a collective responsibility.

(Continued)

(Continued)

Component	Emerging	Accelerating	Mastering
Underperformance is an opportunity for growth, not blame. *(Continued)*	• Performance processes emphasize evaluation with little emphasis on strategies for building capacity. • Interventions, through programs such as turnaround schools, are seen as imposed and punishments.	• Reliance on buying programs, solutions, and external experts is decreasing as internal capacity develops.	• Interventions for underperforming schools are developed as a partnership and focus on capacity building, not buying short-term solutions.
External accountability is used transparently to benchmark progress.	• Standards and expectations for learning, teaching, and leadership are becoming clearer but are not understood or shared by the schools or district. • A culture of competition, not collaboration, is evident. • The school or district overemphasizes negative strategies such as performance appraisal and public ranking of data as incentives for improving performance, rather than using capacity building as the driver for improvement. • Trust is not strong and intervention is viewed as negative.	• The school or district has established standards and expectations for learning, teaching, and leadership, but they may not yet be understood and used consistently. • The school or district is moving to use more capacity-building strategies such as viewing performance appraisal as a vehicle for growth rather than an evaluation. • Data are used more transparently and incorporates measures of organizational health as well as student performance, but the process may not yet be trusted by everyone or used consistently.	• The school or district establishes and promotes professional standards and practices, including performance appraisal. • Data are used transparently and with expertise to improve the learning process at all levels. • Measures of organizational health, student performance, and well-being are monitored. Indictors of organizational health include staff retention rates, leadership turnover rates, teacher absenteeism rates, number of crisis-related incidents, degree of collaboration, and levels of trust. Indicators of student performance and well-being include performance data as well as student sense of control over destiny and engagement in learning.

···
33. Coherence Planning Protocol
···

Purpose

- Develop a 100-Day Plan to increase coherence in your organization.

Link

Reading: Key actions in the Taking Action Protocol and the infographics at the conclusion of each chapter in *Coherence: The Right Drivers in Action for Schools, Districts, and Systems,* by Michael Fullan and Joanne Quinn (Corwin, 2015).

Coherence Planning Protocol

1. Review the results of your Taking Action Protocol key actions for each chapter and your assessment using the Coherence Progression Protocol.

2. Develop 2–3 goal areas that are most crucial to increase coherence in your organization.

3. Identify key actions to take in the next 100 days to move toward the goals. Specify who will take responsibility and the time frame.

4. Review progress and note evidence in the status update column. Use those data to complete the next 100-Day Plan.

Final Thoughts

Coherence comes from ideas and action. Reflect on your situation and where you are in the coherence journey. What are the next steps you could take with your group to achieve greater focus? Remember, coherence is never finished because people come and go, new ideas come along, and the environment changes. But if you follow the framework and its integration, you will always be on the high side of coherence and thus more effective.

---

33. Coherence Planning Protocol (Continued)

Coherence Planning Protocol

1.0 Action Area			
Steps	Lead	Time Frame	Status Update
1.1			
1.2			
1.3			

2.0 Action Area			
Steps	Lead	Time Frame	Status Update
2.1			
2.2			
2.3			

3.0 Action Area			
Steps	Lead	Time Frame	Status Update
3.1			
3.2			
3.3			

References

Borton, T. (1970). *Reach, touch and teach: Student concerns and process education.* New York: McGraw-Hill.

Bruner, J., Goodnow, J. J., & Austin, G. A. (1967). *A study of thinking.* New York: Science Editions.

Fullan, M. (2011, April). *Choosing the wrong drivers for whole system reform.* Centre for Strategic Education. Retrieved from http://www.michaelfullan.ca/media/13396088160.pdf

Fullan, M. (2014, January 21). *Our digital journey: William G. Davis Sr. Public School* [Video file]. Retrieved from http://www.michaelfullan.ca/ontario-wg-davis

Fullan, M. (2014, January 21). *Our journey to awesome: Park Manor Public School* [Video file]. Retrieved from http://www.michaelfullan.ca/ontario-park-manor

Fullan, M. (2014, January 21). *Peel District School Board* [Video file]. Retrieved from https://youtu.be/JV2HYL-WB24

Fullan, M. (2014, January 22). *The perfect storm: Central Peel Secondary School* [Video file]. Retrieved from http://www.michaelfullan.ca/ontario-central-peel

Fullan, M. (2014, May 29). *Our teamwork approach: Peters K–3 Elementary* [Video file]. Retrieved from http://www.michaelfullan.ca/our-teamwork-approach-peters-k-3-elementary

Fullan, M. (2015, February 19). *Topic series 7: Leadership at all levels* [Video file]. Retrieved from http://www.michaelfullan.ca/topic-video-leadership-at-all-levels

Fullan, M. (2015, June 12). *Topic series 19: The push and pull factor* [Video file]. Retrieved from http://www.michaelfullan.ca/topic-video-the-push-pull-factor

Fullan, M., & Quinn, J. (2015). *Coherence: The right drivers in action for schools, districts, and systems.* Thousand Oaks, CA: Corwin.

Google. [Google]. (2014, May 22). *Rubik's cube: A question, waiting to be answered* [Video file]. Retrieved from https://www.youtube.com/watch?v=W1K2jdjLhbo

Gray, J. (2005). *Four "A"s text protocol.* Bloomington, IN: National School Reform Faculty. Harmony Education Center.

Green, S. K., Smith, J., III, & Brown, E. K. (2007). Using quick writes as a classroom assessment tool: Prospects and problems. *Journal of Educational Research & Policy Studies, 7*(2), 38–52.

Hargreaves, A., & Shirley, D. (2009). *The fourth way: The inspiring future for educational change.* Thousand Oaks, CA: Corwin.

Kagan, S. (1989). The structural approach to cooperative learning. *Educational Leadership, 47*(4), 12–15.

Nunan, D. (2003). *Practical English language teaching.* New York: McGraw-Hill.

Palincsar, A. S., & Brown, A. (1984). Reciprocal teaching of comprehension-fostering and comprehension-monitoring activities. *Cognition and Instruction, 1*(2), 117–175.

Short, K., Burke, C., & Harste, J. (1995). *Creating classrooms for authors and inquirers* (2nd ed.). Portsmouth, NH: Heinemann.

Soni, S. [Sumeet Soni]. (2007, December 11). *Be the change that you want to see in this world* [Video file]. Retrieved from https://www.youtube.com/watch?v=nGyutkBvN2s

About the Authors

Social Imagery

Michael Fullan, Order of Canada, is professor emeritus at the Ontario Institute for Studies in Education, University of Toronto. He served as special adviser in education to former premier of Ontario Dalton McGuinty from 2003 to 2013 and now serves as one of four advisers to Premier Kathleen Wynne. Michael has been awarded honorary doctorates from the University of Edinburgh, University of Leicester, Nipissing University, Duquesne University, and the Hong Kong Institute of Education. He consults with governments and school systems in several countries.

Fullan has won numerous awards for his more than thirty books, including the 2015 Grawemeyer Award in Education with Andy Hargreaves for *Professional Capital*. His books include the best sellers *Leading in a Culture of Change, The Six Secrets of Change, Change Leader, All Systems Go, Motion Leadership,* and *The Principal: Three Keys to Maximizing Impact.* His latest books are *Evaluating and Assessing Tools in the Digital Swamp* (with Katelyn Donnelly), *Leadership: Key Competencies for Whole-System Change* (with Lyle Kirtman), *The New Meaning of Educational Change* (5th edition), and *Freedom to Change.* To learn more, visit his website at www.michaelfullan.ca.

Social Imagery

Joanne Quinn is the director of whole system change and capacity building at Michael Fullan Enterprises, where she leads the design of strategic whole system capacity building at the global, national, and district levels. She also serves as the director of global capacity building for New Pedagogies for Deep Learning: A Global Partnership (NPDL), focused on transforming learning. Previously, she provided leadership at all levels of education as a superintendent, implementation adviser to the Ontario Ministry of Education, director of continuing education at the University of Toronto, and special adviser on international projects. She consults internationally on whole system change, capacity building, leadership, and professional learning and is sought by professional organizations and institutions as a consultant, adviser, and speaker. These diverse leadership roles and her passion to improve learning for all give her a unique perspective on influencing positive change.

Jessica Douglas
Photography

Eleanor Adam consults internationally in the areas of leadership, change, and learning and is a senior consultant for the Michael Fullan Enterprises capacity building team. She has worked with educators in several countries and states to improve and deepen learning for all students through excellence in classroom instruction and principal and district leadership. Her recent work has focused on whole system change through the development of coherence at the state and district levels.

She has served as a teacher and principal in both elementary and high schools as well as an acting superintendent and supervisor of special education for a school district. Developing and leading meaningful professional learning is a passion that Eleanor has pursued throughout her career.

Notes

Notes

Notes

Notes

CORWIN

A SAGE Publishing Company

CORWIN HAS ONE MISSION: to enhance education through intentional professional learning.

We build long-term relationships with our authors, educators, clients, and associations who partner with us to develop and continuously improve the best evidence-based practices that establish and support lifelong learning.

ONTARIO PRINCIPALS' COUNCIL

Exemplary Leadership in Public Education

The Ontario Principals' Council (OPC) is a voluntary association for principals and vice-principals in Ontario's public school system. We believe that exemplary leadership results in outstanding schools and improved student achievement. To this end, we foster quality leadership through world-class professional services and supports. As an ISO 9001 registered organization, we are committed to **"quality leadership—our principal product."**